The Purpose of Truth

Also by Gabrielle Journey Jones
and published by Ginninderra Press
Spoken Medicine
Etymology of Courage

Gabrielle Journey Jones

The Purpose of Truth

The Purpose of Truth
ISBN 978 1 76109 573 3
Copyright © text Gabrielle Journey Jones 2023
Cover image: *Yellow for Peace Cottage* by Gabrielle Journey Jones

First published 2023 by
Ginninderra Press
PO Box 3461 Port Adelaide 5015
www.ginninderrapress.com.au

Contents

Foreword	7
On Yuin Country: Acknowledgement of Country – Far South Sketches	
Bemboka	11
Merimbula	12
Tathra	13
Wallaga Lake	14
Impressions	
State of Emergence	17
Walk Slow	19
Driftwood	20
Oakdale Estate, Autumn	21
Redbelly Farm, Winter	23
Fernmark Inn, Spring	24
Peace Cottage, Summer	25
Pieces of Quietude	26
Play Centre Pandemonium	27
Sounds of Home	28
Landing	31
Observations	32
Peppermint Tea	33
Tree Womoon	35
Drum Tonic	36
Fractals of Love	37
Truths	
Dear Journey	41
The Purpose of My Truth	42
What is a Poem?	44
Portable Lives	45

Post Traumatic Relationship Syndrome (PTRS)	46
Gaslit	47
Edges	48
We Are the Sky	49
Labels	50
Decade Dance	52
My World	54

Ekphrasis

River and the Sea Reflections	57
Travellers	58
Watercoloured Words	59
Towards Light	60
Phoenix	61
She Stands	62
Twin Elder Trees	63
Paper Cranes	64
Mandala	65
Guardians	66

Gratitude	67
Acknowledgements	68
About Gabrielle Journey Jones	69

Foreword

it's the details of a thing…what eye love about Gabe's poetry

the depth in the beauty of a moment slowed way down
eye enter her words and the legs of my mind and heart
slow to stroll as eye am carried like a precious thing
on the words of her song…her poetry

from the warm feel of the water on my skin
as a single mother washes the dishes
and sneaks in some dreaming…
to the joy in
'Laughing at gravity with friends
Barrelling down slippery dips'

smile

how she writes my thoughts
she epitomizes what poetry is
texture and color and feelings
and secret thoughts and
the sweet in words that can also sting

these poems are a beautiful carpet ride
through a coloured galaxy that feels
like home to me
and also
some beautiful places eye have not seen
but she makes me feel them
with my heart and also
can rub my hand over all the texture rising
from these pages.

what a beautiful walk this is
and its the kind that doesnt make one tired
and you wanna turn around and do it again
so eye will

E. Nina Jay
Black, Lesbian, Womon, Writer
Chicago, Illinois

On Yuin Country

Acknowledgement of Country – Far South Sketches

Bemboka

Beyond the mountain range
Home of the Djiringanj
Orange flames of sunlight
Trail off on cauliflower clouds.

Our planet slowly turns
Painting her soft belly
In sunset and shadows
Gifting Bemboka another
Wistful fire-tinted winter sky.

Merimbula

Houses carved into headlands
Jut out over the Pacific Ocean
Ancient ritual spaces adjacent
Cleared forests and complacence
This renaissance was not planned
Deeply changing Djiringanj Land.

Rocky waves smash in repetition
Sand waits on storm clouds to open
Seagulls impatient and bold
Swarm Short Point car park
Squawking as vehicles arrive
Lunchtime locals leave behind
Feathers and a hot chip frenzy.

Tathra

Sky and ocean are one
Merging on Tathra Beach
Golden folds of sunset
Reach across the sand
Riding the inbound tide.

Sparkling, the sea yawns
Stretching a fond farewell
To the first day of winter
Sky and ocean are one.

Wallaga Lake

Dancing droplets at dusk
Ripples merge, circles singing
Sprinkled by mirrors of clouds
From summer's watercolour night.

Ashen echoes of an awakening storm
Blue hues of light drawn towards earth
Attention transfixed on gentle rain song
Honouring Gulaga, mother mountain.

Impressions

State of Emergence

Ngunnawal Country was suffocating.
A carbonised container of toxic fumes
Vacuuming in smoke from every direction.
North, raging along the Hume Highway
Scorching the bewildered Southern Highlands
East, fuelled by the fierce Yuin sea breeze
Blazing over rivers, hills and Ngarigo plains
West, billowing across from the Brindabellas
South, sent from the Snowy Mountains inferno.

Stationary in Bega those fiery first days of 2020
Numb with shock as towns around us burned.
Escaping to Canberra felt futile, dangerous.
Holidaymakers abandoned seaside vacations
Fleeing in slow motion on congested country roads.
A 'tourist leave zone' stretched down the South Coast
From Nowra to the no-go state line below Eden
Embers descended terrorising indiscriminately
Flames and fear ripped through brave communities.

Townships we weren't even aware existed
We now know their names, their losses intimately
Illuminated worldwide by the wild Border Fire.
Black Summer seized our complacency
Needlessly, greedily extinguished 33 lives
The smoke swallowed hundreds more over time.

Emergency workers, volunteers and firefighters
United underneath blood orange midday skies
We had been warned by years of extreme weather
Climate change extended fire seasons as predicted
Enduring drought and soaring temperatures
Kindling for lightning strikes and human error.

24 million hectares burnt open a new decade
Ash-clogged waterways are still contaminated
Three billion animals displaced, destroyed, replaced
By an ongoing eerie, silent absence of wildlife.
Mountain tops scalped leaving thin bristles of trees
Like charcoal ghosts dressed in precautionary grief
And buoyant green shoots of regrowth.

Statistics sourced from the Royal Commission into National Natural Disaster Arrangements Report 2020.

Walk Slow

Do not be in such a rush
That you cannot take the path
Through the middle of Littleton Gardens.

Walk slow.

Do not cut across wet grass
Just to get to work faster
Bypassing patches of Yuin sunshine.

Walk slow.

Do not miss the autumn leaves
Swirling their mottled patterns
A gallery of wind blown pavement art.

Walk slow.

Driftwood

Sunshine with a side of wind
An ordinary August weekend
Wandering Mogareeka Inlet
Seabird songs dance and soar
Above these boisterous waves.

Salt-preserved casuarina branches
Travel freely along Bega River estuary
Shelter native vegetation under ageless grace
Protecting plants and sand from coastal erosion
Fascinating, unassuming afterlife of trees.

Driftwood dries on the beach
Bathing in mid-afternoon light
Gathered in improvised bundles
At the whim of the last high tide.

Oakdale Estate, Autumn

A Measure of Contentment

Reflections of the sun ascending
Warm through every glass door and window
With the brightness of familiar smiles
Like the welcome laughter of friendship.

The sound of a tractor purring in the field
Is just a rubbish truck on its unassuming rounds
Soon disappearing down other streets in Nowra Hill.

The wind begins to dance with potted daisies
The succulents refuse to cut in.
Two oak trees sway in the yard
Enjoying the music of morning
Over a choir of pied currawong song.
Autumn is preparing for winter
Brown oak leaves about to fall
Unopened gifts to enrich the soil.

The alabaster moon drifts
Like a hot air balloon
In the ice-blue Yuin sky
Fatigued from performing
Her painted-up blood-red
Lunar eclipse in full bloom.

Four crows caw impatiently
Circling low above the property
A routine sunrise parade
Wings outstretched in unison
A confident display
Their hunt for breakfast
Will find success.

Tiger prowls through long grass
Three years old, stalking imaginary prey
Camouflaged by her dark tortoiseshell coat
Creating adventures under the watchful oak.
Buddy stares outside from the lounge room
Grooming his tufted ebony paws
Envious of his big sister's freedom.
Escape into Cambewarra Mountain
His constant kitten ambition.

Redbelly Farm, Winter

A Measure of Friendship

Window to the crisp blue ocean
Fields of dappled green treetops
Stretch from Redbelly Farm to the sand.
Magpies in the garden sing
Scratching around for breakfast.
Jimmy gingerly patrols the yard
His large Alsatian frame
Scares birds away from plants.
Kelpie pup on his runner lead
Oversees from the balcony
Waiting for Phoenix to rise.
Morning breeze sways rose petals
Lemongrass waves thin long arms
Above mint, strawberries and rhubarb
Rooster's cock-a-doodle call
Crashes through the quiet.
Cold, black charcoal and ashes
Rest in the cast iron cauldron
Underneath the bodhi tree
Retaining memories of close friends
Celebrating winter solstice gratitudes
Pumpkin soup, sticky date pudding
Fire-twirling, music, hugs and laughter.
Intentions released as post-it note wishes
Become cinders and disintegrate
into a star-crowded Djiringanj sky
Riding flame, hope's smoke and pure relief.

Fernmark Inn, Spring

A Measure of Happiness

She made freshly baked banana bread
Warm cups of Australian Afternoon Tea
Shadows cast shapes on blossoming garden beds
Picturesque outside her kitchen window
Unhurried, I contemplate gratitude
For the ease of our closeness.

A rooster echoes across the paddock
Where alpacas and horses retreat
She reclines on a red folding chair
Her laughter buoyant as Fernmark birdsong
Distracting me with her smile
But mostly with her ways of loving
Everyone she cares about so generously.

Her eyes remind me of the sea
On a day as blue and mild as this
Reflected in my dark brown gaze
She is a measure of my happiness.

She loves me like the feeling of home.
She loves me with the radiance of sunshine
Still warming the room after dusk.
She loves me with acres of spaciousness
Found in these foothills of Mumbulla Mountain.

Peace Cottage, Summer

A Measure of Courage

Made a successful offer on my 48th birthday
Two bedrooms and a postage stamp backyard
A vintage rotary clothesline for my children
To swing merrily around on when I'm not looking
As I did in my grandmother's garden.

Lively greenery thriving beneath our silver letterbox
Agapanthus, wiry weeds and wild buffalo grass
Framed by a flaking metal fence and retirement dreams.
A cheery footpath from the iron gate to leaded glass door
Welcomes loved ones to rest awhile at Peace Cottage.
Circa 1935, barely discernible to passers-by with busy lives
Cloaked in beige weatherboards and a rusting tin roof.

A makeshift garage squeezed alongside the house
Sheltering an external laundry under the kitchen window
Chopped wood for the lounge room fireplace
Stacked in an otherwise empty workshop, musty with memories.

My gran used to call her old shed like that a 'lean-to'.
When she reached my age her house had become
A favoured gathering place for family and friends
Gran would have wished this blessing on my first home.

Pieces of Quietude

Unobserved she reclaims
Glistening jewels of time
Hanging out baskets of washing
Leisurely on her clothesline
Pausing to breathe slowly
In the autumn sunshine.
Her day soon explodes with activity
As children tumble out of bed
Solo mumma, perpetually busy
Seeks solitude at the sink
Washing dishes for her family
She gifts herself time to think
Reflecting on the ramshackle
Joys of single-parenthood.

She daydreams while the bath
Fills itself with rainbow bubbles
Her children won't disturb her here
They scatter like supernovae
As bedtime routines begin
She does not bother to call them
Any earlier than absolutely required
Allowing her tired hands to float
Testing the water temperature
Remembering when she soaked
Years ago and found her toes obstructed
Belly bursting with another heartbeat
Swimming in the ocean of her womb.
Ever since, she has been gathering
These sparkling pieces of quietude.

Play Centre Pandemonium

Gleeful, giddy happiness
Tiny faces framed by sweaty hair
Dishevelled clothes and tired smiles
Cartwheels a jumble of arms and legs
Colliding on colourful foam blocks.

Tangle of joyous shrieks
Thunder of toddler feet
Running up bouncy stairs
Laughing at gravity with friends
Barrelling down slippery dips
Manic torpedoes targeting thrills.

Tears of separation
At the sudden awareness
They are completely alone
On top of the rocket ship
Peering out at their people
Little voices echo in unison
'Here I am! Look at me!'

Parents drinking coffee call back
'Just come down if you're scared'
They filter out fun-frenzied children
Returning to the scarce opportunity
For uninterrupted adult conversations.

Sounds of Home

I. Voices

Muffled conversations meandering
From the back bedrooms right through
The thin plasterboard in our cottage
Are comforting thoughts because
They are home, they are safe.

My children coexisting online
Simultaneously with their friends
Sudden screams 'Oh no!' or 'Let's go!'
Followed by wild whoops of congratulations.

Singsong victory dances reverberate
Stomped into carpeted floorboards.
'Turn it down or turn it off' I call out twice
Eventually knocking on shared walls 'It's bedtime.'
'Tuck me in please, Mum! Yes, Simba has been outside.'
'Goodnight, Mum, love you too.'

My darlings now 10 and 13
Becoming themselves
Growing into who they are
Planning their imagined futures
Shining excitement into new ideas.

Reminding me how to love openly
Trusting in each other to thrive.
Attachment parenting
Reverses our familiar roles
I am attached to them
In every letting go.

II. Ten

Counts them on one hand
Her close circle of confidants
No need to divide attention
Between too many companions
'Mum, can my friends come over today?'

Besties hanging at school, home and on social media
Exchanging secrets and weekend plans
Playing games, baking and roller-skating.
Takes her dog for a walk up and down our street
Neighbours wave to my girl and her chihuahua.

Apprentice event managers coordinating sleepovers
Parents are the last to know and first to agree
Grown-up possibilities are daydreamed
Delightfully designing the kind of house
They will all share at eighteen or twenty
Writing new soundtracks for their adult lives.

III. Thirteen

Constantly wondering about life
Confidently asking curious questions
Closely listening for the answers
To add to his own insights.

Five fleeting years until freedom
He can already sense it and prepares.
Independently makes personal choices
About his hairstyle, friends and clothes.

Launches into each day purposefully
A quick breakfast, packs his lunch and school bag
'Love you, Mum, have a really great day'
Bends down for a hug from his soaring height
Glances at the screen and rolls his eyes
Does not want to be part of this poem
Yet he is one of three essential souls
Precious and belonging to our family
Harmonising with our sacred sounds of home.

Landing

My sister warned me
To pack warm clothes
'It's freezing in Melbourne today'
The roads looked like Venice
From the tiny plane
The rain had chosen
Favourite suburbs to torment
In torrents for an entire month.

I looked for blue skies as I always do
The sun appeared to break through
Cloud's thick defence where it could
But the sunbeams were quickly
Swallowed up again.
My sister was right as she usually is.
Icy winds from the South Pole.
Whipped around my ankles
Slapped at my kneecaps
I cursed my cotton slacks.

Along with the inattention to sisterly advice
Denim jeans would have made more sense
As I stepped onto the aluminum stairs
More of a fancy ladder and just as narrow
I self-consciously turned so as not to slip
And create a comic moment in the rain
For all of the people behind me.
Captain nods 'goodbye' as I pass
My face tells him without words
I am so grateful to have landed.

Observations

Her laughter is familiar
Golden and joyful.
Her soul seems soft
Resilient and creative.

Her stories are interwoven
Kind and hopeful.
Her insights are wise
Genuine and practical.

I don't know her very well
Just enough to be curious.
Just enough to believe
What she says about herself.

Peppermint Tea

Sunday afternoon sky overcast
Lounging, live music floats high
Above another eco festival by the sea.
A lavish lunch of ice cream treats
Wrapped in fancy waffles, gluten free.
A reusable red floral paper cup
Lukewarm with peppermint tea
Helped to settle my stomach
Just as she suggested it would.

It's a pleasure to be in her presence
Like an old mate I've known for years
We create an easy space to listen
With encouragement and optimism.
We seem to have so much in common
As we exchange our observations
Life theories planting new shoots
A sapling that might grow to become
A shady casuarina or an ageing ghost gum
Roots connected beneath the surface
Deeply grounding a new friendship.

The chrysalis of a creative spark, vulnerable
To miscommunication, misinterpretation
Scarcity surrounding 'not enough time'.
There is faerie magic in how diaries
Open up perfectly for the right people.
We find room in overscheduled lives
Already filled with happiness and love
We choose to practise trust
Sharing stories on a picnic rug
Sipping our peppermint tea
As a local band plays funk rhythms
Singing about saving the trees.

Tathra Eternity Festival 2022

Tree Womoon

Her phone is switched off
So she can tune in to herself
No one reaching in to distract
From her task of simply being.
Sacred time alone and with family
She will celebrate 55 in nature's embrace.

I imagine there will be tears
Of insight, gratitude and grief
Outstretching deep feelings
As qigong reconnects her body
From her crown chakra down
To her feet, grounded like tree roots
Anchored in Aboriginal Land
Ngarigo Country near the river
This ancient place now holds her, home.

I hear the song her heart sings
In English and in her mother tongue
Far from the Bavarian soil she grew up on
A mixture of chant and hope
Story, release and creativity
She moves colours from her mind
To every blank canvas she prepares
Her thoughts a brilliant palette
Refined through 55 years of artistry.

Drum Tonic

She listens.
Her attention connected
Inside the djembe drumbeat.
Her own unique heartbeat
Synchronising with the rhythms
As she listens.

She smiles.
Her joyfulness reflected
Inside the djembe drumbeat.
Her own unique heartbeat
Synchronising with the rhythms
As she smiles.

She dances.
Her body reconnected
Inside the djembe drumbeat.
Her own unique heartbeat
Synchronising with the rhythms
As she dances.

She merges.
Her soul deepens perspective
Inside the djembe drumbeat.
Her own unique heartbeat
Synchronising with the rhythms
As she merges.

Fractals of Love

Cherished things
Mostly treasured memories
Laughter, songs, earrings
Happiness and poetry
Funny little inside jokes
Once intimately spoken.
Today is an anniversary
I choose to celebrate
With both gratitude and regret
Fractals of love are colourful
Reminders that in meeting you
My journey was deeply blessed.

Truths

Dear Journey

As a child you were fearless
Independent, strong-willed
Believing yourself unstoppable
Certain that you understood
How to harness the magic of life.

You would daydream while stuck inside
Gazing through cold Canberra windows
Frost on the glass an accomplice
Complex scenarios mapped in detail
Milestone activities premeditated
Logistics and contingencies covered
You would attempt every idea
Perceived worthy of action
Inviting friends on escapades
For their laughter and company.

You could envision anything
Then one task at a time
Without fuss it would be done.
Those same ideals follow you
50 laps around the sparkling sun.
A passion for sharing adventures
Co-creating community to renew
Faith in humanity and a life of magic.

The Purpose of My Truth

I've been writing rhymes since 1979
To tell myself the truth
And let the telling unbind me.

Don't bind me in binaries
Trying to define me
Accept me as you find me!
I reject a shallow narrow
Either/or reality.
I see self-expression
As the key to integrity
It's not for you to say
Who I am
or who I should be.

I welcomed you
You welcome me
Inclusion and equality
Is the essence of community
That's common sense
If we use all of our senses
Intuitive perceptions
Will help us if we let them.

If you tell yourself the truth
Be careful who's around you
Make sure you are seen
You are heard and valued
Ditch haters if you have to
Dictators never love you
They label and enslave to
Keep you from your own truth!
I tell myself the truth
And let the telling unbind me
The purpose of my truth
Is to remind me
Why I have to speak.

What is a Poem?

Poems are time capsules
Opened every time they are read
Poems are love letters
To exes and also to friends
Poems cradle secrets
Inside the light they shed
Poems are doorways
To the soul laid bare.

A poem is a universal prayer
A poem is a safe place to share
A poem is a gentle high-five mid-air
A poem is a favourite comfy chair.

A poem kindly notices you are there
A poem is compassionate self-care
A poem reconnects heart and head
A poem makes art of stories bled.

Portable Lives

Some houses have an entire junk room
We only have room for junk boxes
Treasured chests and old suitcases
Salvaged from the shipwreck of separation
Containers of collected experiences.

Like the eventual death of our family
Station wagon, all of her familiar contents
Swept into a coffin of a cardboard box
Memorialised now beside my bed
Hidden with six others underneath
An ink-stained rainbow tablecloth
Storage imitating furniture perfectly
Balancing a lamp, scrap paper and a leaky pen.

There is a plastic box crammed with school reports
Notebooks, kindergarten drawings and newsletters
Memories held for my children to enjoy
When we have a permanent place to unpack.
Another tattered box rattles with rainy day activities
Miscellaneous things like old jewellery and crystals
Messy art supplies, birthday cards and missing keys
Overcrowded with creativity and melancholy.

Three other cartons remain sealed
Four decades folded up carefully
Our portable lives held closely
Inside these precious junk boxes
Waiting for us to find home and safety.

Post Traumatic Relationship Syndrome (PTRS)

Pretend you're okay
Tell no one the truth
Relinquish identity
Stay small and silent.

Plan your escape
Try a few hundred times
Resist in secret ways
Scared and compliant.

People will help
This pain will pass
Re-enter the world
Solid steps of resilience.

Prepare your allies
Talk about defence
Reorganise your energy
Stage your insurgence.

Prioritise your safety
Trust your intuition
Realise your worth
Survive domestic violence.

Gaslit

They fashion
Makeshift weapons
From your unsuspecting words
Whatever you dare to say
Is used to beat you down
As if you attacked yourself.
Silence is what saves you.

They think
No one will believe you
They ensure you're isolated
Remove your safest places
Favourite people first.
You imagine you're alone
Then they attempt their worst.

They want
Their actions to hurt
Emotional violators
Coercive control abuse
Is not a new method
to redefine your truth.
Compliance is what hides you.

Edges

Edge of lake
Edge of tears
Edge of comfort
Edge of queer.

Two-edged sword
Two-way street
Two-spirited souls
Twofold relief.

Folded arms
Folded hearts
Folded stories
Folded cards.

Cards held close
Cards ignored
Cards unplayed
Cards over-thought.

Overexposed
Overcome patterns
Overtly content
Overdue joy.

We Are the Sky

We are not the storm
We are the sky
Stretching forever blue
Above this dark amassing cloud
Pregnant with yesterday's grief.

We are not the storm
We are the sky
A kaleidoscopic canvas
Depicting peace and hope
Within a single sunbeam.

We are not the storm
We are the sky
Allowing the essence of our lives
To dance joy into existence
Under universal encouragement.

Labels

My doctor diagnosed
Me with Labels
Said I got a bad case
Of the Labels
Labels I can live with
With a bit of stigma
Titrated medication
And some laxatives.

My doctor didn't want to be
Too prescriptive
Referred me to a Shrink
Who could fix this
Psych-analysis was swift
Told me I will be OK
If I learn to outlive
These labels.

Checked on my schedule
We can do a fortnightly zoom
Empty my head full of Labels
Deconstruct the narratives
That inform the adjectives
Written on my forms
Professionals are sure
If we talk it out some more
Together we can heal these labels.

Peel these labels
Off once and for all
Watch them fall into the past
Like the bad memories they are
They won't ever leave a scar
When I've learned to outlive
These labels.

Decade Dance

In your fifties
You no longer
Talk about
Your grandmother.
Your children
Never knew her
They are grown
And are too busy
For your childhood
Memories.

In your fifties
You might become
A grandmother
Sharing stories
Weaving your family tree
Constellations set free
For your grandchildren
To dance with in dreams.

In your fifties
You think about
Your ancestors
You listen carefully
For their tribal drums
The splash of ocean
Against wooden canoes
A pan flute and harp
Maybe bagpipes on the wind
Reminding you the direction home
Though it's not yet time to go.

In your fifties
Wisdom gathered
Guides you gently
Feeling the fragile
Balance of the veil
Loss accelerates
Loved ones cross too soon
Leaving us behind
Finding gratitude within
The hidden gifts of time
Half a century of life.

My World

Poetry my truth
Drumming my pulse
Ocean my blood
Sky my freedom.

Family my life
Love my purpose
Connection my vision
Joy my mission.

Brown my skin
Golden my soul
Trusting my eyes
Welcoming my hug.

Malleable my heart
Careful my words
Close my circle
Safe my home.

Ekphrasis

River and the Sea Reflections

Uncle Ben's birds-eye brushstrokes
Blessed many of his subjects unaware
That he was painting them into forever.
Crafted landscapes on Yuin Nation
Sunshine swirled across canvas
Illuminating candid conversations
Between mountains and ocean
Whispered along the river tracing
Umbarra Black Duck Songlines.

Bejewelled butterflies glisten
Bedazzling busy billabongs
Cockatoos circle contributing
Equal gifts friendship and feathers
Dancing kangaroos in flight
Dingoes and wallabies harmonise
Snakes warm themselves in good weather
Lazy geese swim, glide and dive
A kaleidoscope of wildlife.

People sway in patterned pairs
Entranced on a disco dance floor
An intimate affair capturing
A collection of favourite memories
Each couple a sacred story
Unfolding within Uncle's narrative.
Perhaps, earlier that day they lined the sand
Preparing to have a go at beach volleyball
Socially distanced like a string of Christmas lights.

Travellers

Silence is fertile soil
To grow seeds of peace
It does not take long
Before they are released
Graceful as they dance
Away from flower husks
Waiting on the unseen wind
Courageous travellers.

Heading for the stars
Into chartless galaxies
Lightness and simplicity
Open to unknown destiny
Teaching us how to flow
'One' with each other
Connected with harmony
Remembering to dance.

Watercoloured Words

Watercoloured words
Sweeping across a fresh canvas
Drip-painted bright powerful
Letters dropped onto a page
Forming all shades of poetry
Literary and fine arts collaborate
Creating true mixed media
Constructing vibrant new expressions
For eyes, ears and hearts to contemplate.

Towards Light

Travelling at a steady pace towards the light
Transitioning from a cosy, quiet cave
Into the luminous exposure
Of a scorching Australian desert heat
Without any need for shade
Fresh ideas brought willingly to consciousness
Promises to self of new beginnings
Expectations of transformational change
Unfurling newborn butterfly wings in the sun
Unfettered courage to take to the air
Fluttering into the magnetic
Fire-yellow glow beckoning.

Phoenix

Take a rainbow carpet ride
Kaleidoscope of colours
Cascade, tumble, collide
Fireworks ignited to hypnotise
Unapologetic celebration of life
An open invitation to fly
To be creatively inspired.

Look closer
Watch the phoenix dive
Swooping low with calculating eyes
Wings ablaze dazzling spectral shine
Centring herself as she prepares to rise.
Regenerating artistic sparks
From the heart of where imagination resides.

Behold the birthplace
Of creative expression
Limitless source of inspiration
Elliptical fountain overflowing
An abundance of joy
Each shiny whirling particle
Radiating infinite possibilities.

She Stands

She stands confident that
One fearless woman
Dancing into the unknown
Can inspire generations.

She stands listening for the rhythms
Of Mother Earth's heartbeat drum
Poised with open arms to move
In synchronicity with Gaia.

She stands in solidarity
With those brave enough
To cast off indifference
And release the power
Of unthinkable truths.

She stands offering
To heal her world
Through loving connections
One friend at a time
Beginning with herself.

Twin Elder Trees

A patch of sunlight where night has been
Mirage shimmers like the moon descending
Brightly washing over hot thirsty terrain.
Desert song travels the morning breeze
Lifting leaves, loosening their melodies
Gently shaking free natural harmonies
Siphoned through twin elder trees
Gifting life with playful spontaneity.

Paper Cranes

The remnants of one thousand paper cranes
A floating origami tsunami
Sweeping along the swollen golden river
Carrying with them unwavering hope
That a desperate wish will be granted
By the mystical creatures of Senbazuru legend.

If we could change our fate with simple acts
Of folded paper, faith and whispered prayers
Would a lot more trees sacrifice themselves for humanity?
And would we, in return, wish for something less personal?

Mandala

Magnificent mandala
Of fractured light
Tracing a labyrinth
Along charcoaled pathways
As if chasing the Sun
To her setting place
Never quite catching up.

The Earth circles
Bewitched by her
Mesmerising luminosity
Capturing only rainbows
Lucky pots of gold
Clutching them deeply
Into the heart of
Its ragged starry night.

A tactile treasure map
Of visual wonderment
For soft eyes and careful hands
Spinning a colour wheel
Seven layers wide
Every individual piece
Happily vibrating
In an unconscious oneness
With the whole.

Guardians

Guardians of creative fire
Gather at the luminous pool
Enchanted by iridescent waters
Swirling rhythmically in the moonlight
On a late autumn evening.

A peaceful, hopeful meeting begins
Standing in circle formation
Everyone equal, every opinion
Welcome and respected
Intergenerational way-finding
A mutual exchange as elders
Garner knowledge from their youth
Wisdom found in collective listening.

The glow of this gentle communion
Moves purposefully in golden waves
Surrounding billabong conversations
Ancestors have met for millennia
At this same sacred place
Ever-present in the deep green
Blueness of the darkening night.

Gratitude

This collection was collated and edited on Djiringanj Land, Yuin Country, Far South Coast NSW, Australia. Always was and always will be Aboriginal land. Much appreciation to Ginninderra Press for the opportunity to be part of their diverse, welcoming poetry community. Special thanks to Leah Szántó, editor at Final Proof, for her care and precise attention to detail with this collection.

For their words of support and time taken to read my manuscript, thank you my sisters E Nina Jay and Vanessa Lee-Ah Mat. Your poetry guides me deeper into self-compassion and your courage is my community. Morgan Morganics Lewis, thank you for your reflections on this book. I have long respected your word craft and work in the Australian hip hop scene, amplifying voices in remote communities. Eternal friendship and gratitude to Julia Jacobs for our work together on Art Sparks, her paintings from 2012 to 2013 inspiring the final eight poems of this book, exploring truth through ekphrasis.

My love and gratitude for my children Jai, Sofara and my niece Winnie May for their enthusiasm and patience with my performance rehearsals. To my mum Patricia Jones for always being there for us. I appreciate how my family and close friends support and inspire my creative curiosity and truth-speaking through poetry.

> 'Tell your own truths.
> You are the one who knows them best.'
> – Gabrielle Journey Jones

Acknowledgements

'On Yuin Country' is also published in *Legacies* (2021) by South Coast Writers Centre.
'Peace Cottage' is also published in *Milestones* (2021) by Ginninderra Press.
'Pieces of Quietude' is also published in *Women of Words* (2022) by Ginninderra Press.
'Play Centre Pandemonium' is also published in *Shoot the Breeze* (2022) anthology by Girls on Key Poetry.
'Post Traumatic Relationship Syndrome (PTRS)', 'Gaslit' and 'Edges' are also published in *Admissions: Voices within mental health* (2022) a MAD poetry anthology by Upswell Publishing.
'What is a Poem?' and 'Labels' are also published in Westwords anthology *Silence Transformed* (2023).
'Portable Lives' is also published in *Borderless: a transnational anthology of feminist poetry* (2021) by Recent Work Press.
'River and the Sea Reflections' is also published in *Mantle* (2022) by the South Coast Writers Centre.
'Travellers' was inspired by artwork *Dance of Life* by Alena Kennedy, published in Symphony Exhibition e-catalogue (2017).

The final eight poems in this book were written as part of Art Sparks – Poetry and Paint, a project inspired by the work of visual artist Julia Jacobs in response to Gabrielle's poetry (2012–13).

About Gabrielle Journey Jones

Gabrielle Journey Jones is a poet, percussionist, event producer and social worker born on sovereign Gadigal Land, Sydney, Australia. She is from Māori and African American bloodlines and has lived in Bega on Djiringanj Land with her family since 2018. Gabrielle has shared her poetry at local, national and international events for thirty years.

Gabrielle is inspired by trauma-sensitive creative communities which celebrate diversity, activism and inclusion. She encourages everyone to speak their own medicine by sharing their stories and truths in whatever ways feel healing, authentic and meaningful. Gabrielle has two other poetry collections published by Ginninderra Press, *Etymology of Courage* (2021) and *Spoken Medicine* (2017).

Visit linktr.ee/gabriellejourney

www.ingramcontent.com/pod-product-compliance
Lightning Source LLC
Chambersburg PA
CBHW071033080526
44587CB00015B/2601